MW01225350

Peru is a country in South America.

It's Capital is Lima.

PERU has about 32 million people (about the same as California).

Peru is about size of Maine, Texas, New York and California combined.
The official language is Spanish

Lima, Peru

Spanish is the official language of Peru.

Number	Spanish
0	Cero
1	Uno
2	Dos
3	Tres
4	Cuatro
5	Cinco
6	Seis
7	Siete
8	Ocho
9	Nueve
10	Diez

Climate in Peru varies greatly. The coastal areas are mostly a warm tropical climate. Peru has a large 1500 mile long coastline. The Sechura desert borders the coastline. Many small rivers run through the desert making it good growing area for many crops. In 1728, The town of Sechura was destroyed by a Tsunami and was later rebuilt at its current location.

The region with the Andes mountains is much colder than the coastal regions. The Andes are the longest continental mountain range in the world. It is 4300 miles long and has an average height of 13,000 ft. They are the worlds second highest mountain range. Besides being stunningly beautiful, the Andes Mountains in Peru provide lots of attractions, from historical ruins, to charming mountain towns. Many Andes Mountain natives still dress in traditional garments, and in Peru, the descendants of the mighty Inca are among the most colorful people you will find anywhere on the planet.

The margay is very similar to the larger ocelot in appearance, although the head is a little shorter, the eyes larger, and the tail and legs longer. Margay prefers life in rainforests, deciduous and evergreen forests, but it can be also spotted near the coffee and cocoa plantations. Margay is shy animal that avoid people and exact number of remaining animals in the wild is unknown. Unlike other cats, margay is able to move down the tree, with its head going before feet (like squirrels). This is possible because it has flexible ankles of the front feet that can be rotated for 180 degrees.

Tayras are long, slender animals with an appearance similar to weasels. They can grow to be over 15 pounds. Tayra is a very agile creature. It is able to walk and climb skillfully like a cat on the ground and to swim like a fish when it is in the water. Tayra has very long and sharp claws that are used for climbing. They are active at night. Tayra is a vocal animal that uses different sounds for communication. Yowls, snarls and clicking noise are just some of the sounds used for communication in the group.

Adult bush dogs have soft long brownish-tan fur, with a lighter reddish tinge on the head, neck and back and a bushy tail, while the underside is dark, sometimes with a lighter throat patch. Younger individuals, however, have black fur over their entire bodies. Bush dogs are carnivores and hunt during the day. . Although they can hunt alone, bush dogs are usually found in small packs. The dogs can bring down much larger prey. When hunting prey, part of the pack chases it on land, and part wait for it in the water, where it often retreats.

The giant anteater, also known as the ant bear, is a large insectivorous mammal native to Central and South America. They can weigh up to 90 pounds. Anteaters are have no teeth. But their long tongues are more than sufficient to lap up the 35,000 ants and termites they swallow whole each day. The giant anteater can reach 7 feet long from the tip of its snout to the end of its tail

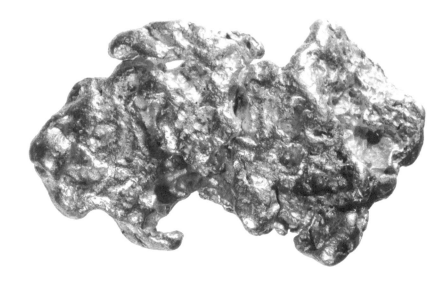

Gold is a major export of Peru. Gold is used not only in jewelry but also in many computers and electronics. Yanacocha gold mine is located in the province and department of Cajamarca Region, about 800 kilometers northeast of Lima, Peru in the Northern highlands at 3,500 and 4,100 meters above sea level. It operates in four primary basins and is the largest gold mine in South America and the 4th largest gold mine in the world.

Copper ore is a major export of Peru. Copper is commonly used to make pipes, coins and wires. Peru is the second largest producer of copper and the government is investing on helping the industry expand further. Archaeologists believe it may be the first metal ever used by man. More than 10,000 years ago, natural deposits of "native copper" were discovered on the surface of the Earth. The people of that time learned that this newfound material could be fashioned into knives, axes and other tools much easier than the tools they were making out of stone. For nearly five thousand years afterward, copper was the only metal known to primitive man.

Peru exports large amounts of zinc. Pure zinc is a shiny bluish-white colored metal. An important quality of zinc is its ability to resist corrosion and therefore protect other metals. Half of all zinc produced today is used to galvanize steel to prevent against corrosion. It is used to protect buildings, cars, nails, wire, pipes and more. Zinc compounds such as zinc oxide are found in many common commercial products, including batteries, paint, plastics, rubber products, pharmaceuticals, floor coverings, inks, cosmetics, soap, and textiles. Zinc is also a natural insect repellent and sun screen, helping to protect our skin.

Most of the guinea pigs people have for pets originated in Peru. Peru exports guinea pigs throughout the world. Did you know that doctors in the Andes mountains in South America have been known to use guinea pigs to find illnesses in people? What they do is to put the guinea pig up against the sick person and it will let out a squeak when they close to where the disease is. Guinea pigs can live on their own after 5 days. In the wild they travel in herds.

In Peru and other South American countries, guinea pigs are eaten as food.

This is San Martin Square in Lima Peru. This beautiful square expresses the grandeur and solidity of independent Peru and that is why every element that compounds it has a monumental aspect. It has colorful gardens, bronze lanterns, marble benches, granite floor, it also has four water fountains on the corners of the square and in the central part, the monument to Don Jose de San Martin. Among the big buildings that surround the square, we can find: Colón theater, Giacoletti building, Bolivar Hotel, Zela and Pumacahua portals and Metro cinema, and some other buildings that make it one of the most beautiful squares of Lima.

Hotels often bill themselves as the most luxurious, the largest, the newest, but it's not often they can claim this one: tallest building in the country. That would be the Westin Hotel in Lima, which is the highest skyscraper in Peru. At 120 meters, it towers over pretty much everything.

Located in the San Isidro business and financial district, the Westin Lima Hotel & Conference center also boasts what is considered to be the best convention facilities in South America.

The Government Palace is an especially historical landmark and has been updated and rebuilt a number of times over the years. It serves as the home for the President of Peru.

The Government Palace was built by Francisco Pizarro, the governor of New Castile. The palace has several ceremonial rooms. There is a well-kept garden in the same place that the Spanish conqueror wanted it to be. The legend affirms that a fig tree log reached Pizarro's hands and that he planted and took care of it. It grew and the same tree, challenging time, is still alive in the place.

Chan Chan is the largest known Pre-Columbian city in South America,. The City was built from adobe (clay). It flourished in 850 -- 1470 AD. Chan Chan consists of 10 walled citadels.

Ciudadelas were large architectural masterpieces which housed plazas, storerooms, and burial platforms for the royals. The splendor of these ciudadelas suggests their association with the royal class. Housing for the lower classes of Chan Chan's hierarchical society are known as small, irregular agglutinated rooms . Because the lower classes were often artisans whose role in the empire was to produce crafts, many of these rooms were used as workshops.

Sapo is a coin-tossing game in which the players try to toss a coin into holes on top of a box. There is also a frog on top of the box, and if a coin gets into the frog's mouth, that player is the winner. If no coin goes into the frog's mouth, the players toss all of their coins and then take the total of the boxes in which they have landed. This game is derived from a traditional Peruvian game.

Kina Malpartida is a big star in Peru and a big deal on the professional women's boxing scene. In terms of popularity, she sits quite comfortably among the top five stars from the world of contemporary Peruvian sports, as well as being one of the most famous people from Peru on the world stage. Considering that Malpartida is one of very few world champions that Peru can currently lay claim to, her celebrity status is understandable and more than deserved.

Carlos Ismael Noriega (born 1959) is a Peruvian and U.S. citizen, NASA employee, a former NASA astronaut and a retired U.S. Marine Corps lieutenant colonel. Noriega reported to the Johnson Space Center in March 1995. He completed a year of training and evaluation, and was qualified for assignment as a mission specialist in May 1996. He held technical assignments in the Astronaut Office EVA/Robotics and Operations Planning Branches. Noriega flew on STS-84 in 1997 and STS-97 in 2000. He has logged over 461 hours in space including over 19 hours in 3 space walks.

Peru's earliest artwork came from the Cupisnique culture, which was concentrated on the Pacific coast, and the Chavín culture. The artists worked with gold, silver, and ceramics to create a variety of sculpture and relief carvings. These civilizations were also known for their architecture and stone sculpture.

The Cuzco School of the early 16th Century incorporated native Peruvian artists, especially Quechua, and imitated the European style of drawing and oil-painting, with religious themes. Diego Quispe Tito emerged during this period, and is still today a revered Peruvian artist. He was one of the most famous Peruvian painters in the Cuzco School tradition. Ignacio Merino was one of the Peruvian artists who best captured the trend for French Romanticism in the 19th century, and modern day Peruvian art continues to be influenced by its indigenous heritage.

Refrigerated Strawberry Cheese-cake

Ingredients:
2 cups ground vanilla cookies (or Graham crackers)
½ cup butter, melted
1 (14-oz) can sweetened condensed milk
1 (8-oz) package cream cheese, at room temperature
Juice of three lemons
2 lb strawberries
4-5 tablespoons sugar
¾ cup orange juice
1 teaspoon potato starch

Directions:

Preheat the oven to 350° F.

Combine the vanilla cookies with the butter. Put the mixture in the base of a pie pan and push with your fingers until it is uniform. Bake for 10 to 15 minutes or until the cookies are lightly golden. Cool in a rack.

Pour the sweetened condensed milk and the cream cheese into a bowl, and beat with a mixer until smooth and creamy. Add the lemon juice and stir with until the cream becomes thicker.

Pour the mixture over the cookie crust and refrigerate.

To make the berry sauce: cook half of the strawberries in a saucepan with the sugar over medium heat. Stir until the berries release their juices. Add the orange juice and bring to a boil for 5 minutes. Strain the mixture, pressing the fruit in the sieve. Discard the solids and pour the juice back into the saucepan.

Dissolve the potato starch in ½ cup water and add to the sauce. Stir and simmer over medium heat until it boils. Transfer to a jar or a saucer, and cool completely.

Slice the remaining strawberries and place them on top of the cheesecake. Refrigerate the cheesecake for a couple of hours. Drizzle with berry sauce.

Machu Picchu is evidence of the urban Inca Empire at the peak of its power and achievement—a city of cut stone fit together without mortar so tightly that its cracks still can't be penetrated by a knife blade. The complex of palaces and plazas, temples and homes may have been built as a ceremonial site, a military stronghold, or a retreat for ruling elites. Built without the use of mortar, metal tools, or the wheel, Machu Picchu stands as an archaeological wonder of the ancient world.

The Nazca Lines are a series of large ancient geo-
glyphs in the Nazca Desert, in southern Peru. The
largest figures are up to 1,200 ft. long. The figures
vary in complexity. Hundreds are simple lines and
geometric shapes; more than 70 are designs of animals, such as birds, fish, llamas, jaguars, and mon-
keys, or human figures. Other designs include trees
and flowers. It is not known how or why these im-
ages were created but they are estimated to be
1500 or more years old.

Printed in the USA
CPSIA information can be obtained
at www.ICGtesting.com
LVHW070237090424
776844LV00019B/43